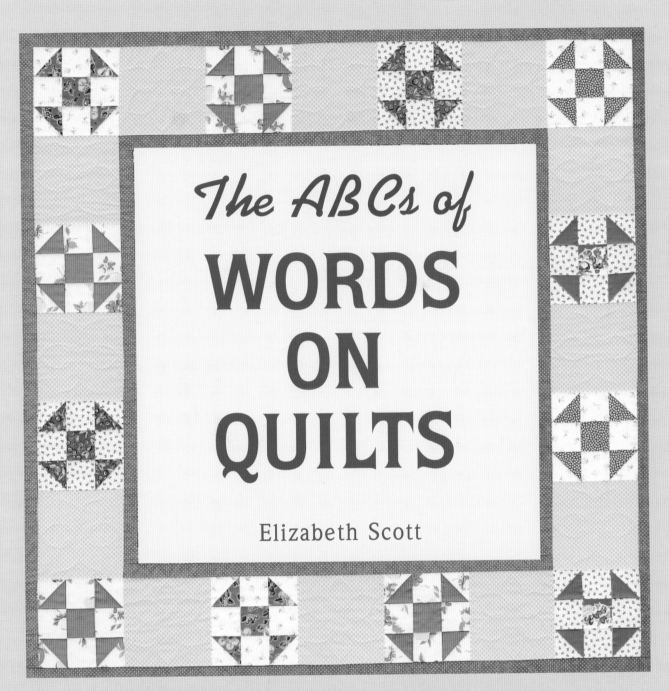

The ABCs of
WORDS
ON
QUILTS

Elizabeth Scott

Appliqué & Embroidery Lettering Techniques
Beautiful Projects • 6 Complete Alphabets

C&T PUBLISHING

Text © 2007 Elizabeth Scott

Artwork © 2007 C&T Publishing, Inc.

Publisher: Amy Marson

Editorial Director: Gailen Runge

Acquisitions Editor: Jan Grigsby

Editor: Liz Aneloski

Technical Editors: Helen Frost and Carolyn Aune

Copyeditor/Proofreader: Wordfirm Inc.

Cover Designer: Kristy Zacharias

Book Designer: Rose Sheifer-Wright

Illustrator: Kirstie L. Pettersen

Production Coordinator: Kerry Graham

Photography by C&T Publishing, Inc., unless otherwise noted

Published by C&T Publishing, Inc., P.O. Box 1456, Lafayette, CA 94549

Library of Congress Cataloging-in-Publication Data

Scott, Elizabeth.

The ABCs of words on quilts : - applique & embroidery lettering techniques, - beautiful projects, - 6 complete alphabets / Elizabeth Scott.

p. cm.

Includes index.

ISBN-13: 978-1-57120-371-7 (paper trade : alk. paper)

ISBN-10: 1-57120-371-0 (paper trade : alk. paper)

1. Quilting--Patterns. 2. Appliqué--Patterns. 3. Embroidery--Patterns. I. Title.

TT835.S359155 2007

746.46'041--dc22

2006031553

Printed in China

10 9 8 7 6 5 4 3 2 1

Acknowledgments

Thank you to:

Alex Anderson, a mentor and friend who helped me believe I could do this;

Leslie and Melissa Emery, who through their wonderful quilt shop, In Between Stitches in Livermore, California, have provided friendship and encouragement;

Pam Vieira-McGinnis, whose friendship and enthusiasm bring so much to my life;

Moda/United Notions for being so generous with their beautiful fabric;

and finally to my family, Larry, Eric, Nick, and Jeff, for their love and support.

Table of Contents

Introduction

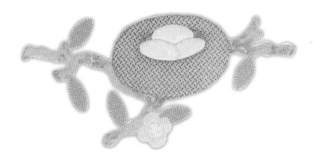

I love making quilts!

There's something almost magical about the way fabric and creativity combine to result in something that can provide warmth and comfort, as well as delight the eye. The personal nature of quilts is a big part of their charm.

Whether you are creating a quilt to toss over your couch, hang on your wall, or wrap around a new baby, you take the time to choose just the right design, colors, and fabric for your project. But why be limited by commercial patterns? The addition of lettering in the style of your choosing can make an ordinary quilt unique and extra special.

Almost any quilt pattern can be personalized with lettering. A verse or favorite quote can be added to the border of a pieced quilt, and for appliqué quilts the possibilities are endless! A flowing banner or ribbon can have lettering embroidered on it. Or words can be freely applied to the background of an appliqué block.

I have provided several alphabets to get you started. There are many sources for interesting fonts that are easily accessible to any quiltmaker, and the knowledge of a few tips and techniques makes it easy to add these letters to your quilts.

My preferred method of appliqué is to use fusible web to secure the appliqué pieces onto the background fabric and a machine blanket stitch to permanently attach them. All the quilts in this book were constructed using this method. Once you've added lettering to a quilt, you will come up with ideas for other projects. Maybe you have names and dates that you'd like to add to personalize a wedding or baby quilt. Perhaps you have a favorite quote that you'd like to add to a project for a friend. Any quilt can be made more special with the addition of beautiful lettering.

So let's get started!

Tools and Supplies

Fabric

It is important to work with only high-quality, 100% cotton fabric. Not only is good fabric easier to work with, but you (and the quilt's recipient) will want your heirloom to last for years.

I recommend prewashing all of your fabrics. This step will eliminate the danger of excess shrinkage and bleeding of dyes. Prewashing will also remove any chemical residue that may keep your fabrics from adhering properly to the fusible web.

When choosing fabrics for your project, it is important to include fabrics of different values (lights and darks) so you will have enough contrast to make your lettering show up against your background fabric.

Examples of value differences in fabric—from light to dark

You can use solid-color fabrics for your letters, as I did on *La Vie en Rose* (page 54) and *Garden Fresh* (page 65), or you can use tone-on-tone prints to add a more elegant look to your lettering, as seen on *Home and Family* (page 24).

Solid-color lettering; detail *La Vie en Rose*

Solid-color lettering; detail *Garden Fresh*

Tone-on-tone lettering; detail *Home and Family*

I had fun using a small-scale floral print for my *Spring Runner* (page 37). Prints can add zip to your project as long as they aren't so busy that they would be visually distracting.

Use of print fabric in lettering; detail *Spring Runner*

The most common choice is to use darker lettering on a lighter background, but the reverse can be especially interesting, as on *Happily Ever After* (page 42).

Light lettering on darker background; detail *Happily Ever After*

Thread

I prefer 100% cotton, 50-weight thread for piecing, appliqué, and machine quilting. A neutral tan is perfect for piecing. For appliqué, I like to match my thread color to the color of the appliqué pieces. For a different look, consider using a contrasting thread. Black blanket stitching, for example, will give your quilt a folk-art flavor. Choosing one color for all your blanket stitching will also save time! For hand embroidery, I use two strands of embroidery floss.

Needles

For machine blanket-stitch appliqué, my favorite needle is a Schmetz Microtex Sharp size 80/12.

For hand embroidery, the right needle is a personal choice. To get the best looking stitches, you'll want to use the thinnest and sharpest needle you're comfortable with. I like a sharps or straw needle size 10, but many people find an embroidery needle easier to work with. Start with the smallest needle you can thread without difficulty.

Tip: A desktop needle threader is an invaluable tool for saving time and your eyesight.

Presser Foot

For blanket stitching, I like an open-toe presser foot. It allows you to more easily see your work as you stitch.

Open-toe presser foot

Fusible Web

I love to appliqué with fusible web. It's fast and easy, and it gives me the old-fashioned look I love.

There are several brands of fusible web on the market, so experiment to see which product you like best. Choose a lightweight fusible web so that your appliqué will not look or feel stiff when the quilt is finished. I prefer Lite Steam-A-Seam 2 by The Warm Company for my projects.

Marking Tools

For tracing appliqué motifs onto fusible web, I prefer to use a black Sharpie Ultra Fine Point marker. For embroidery I like to use a silver Verithin pencil or (if I'm feeling brave!) a Pigma Micron pen in a color close to the color of the embroidery floss. Be sure to heat set the ink with your iron before stitching if you choose this method. For drawing guidelines, I use an air- or water-erasable fabric marker.

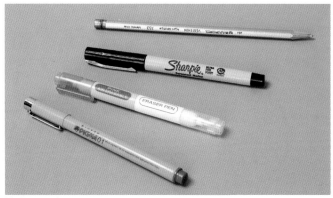

Marking tools

Scissors

You will need three pairs of scissors: one for snipping thread and embroidery floss, one for cutting paper, and one for cutting out your appliqué pieces. Cutting through fusible web can dull your scissors, so I recommend dedicating a pair for that purpose. They need to be sharp enough and small enough to make intricate cuts, but they don't have to be expensive.

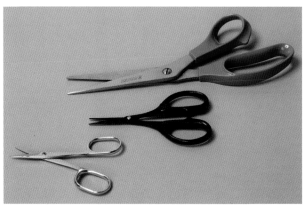

Scissors

Additional Helpful Items

Tracing paper is invaluable for auditioning designs, adjusting letters, and tracing the letters for your projects. You have to trace the mirror image of the letter onto your fusible web, and tracing paper makes this process easy. Just trace the right side of the letter onto the tracing paper and flip the tracing over when it's time to transfer the design to the fusible web.

A lightbox makes tracing motifs easy and is great for helping to decide where to place your appliqué pieces onto your fabric. If you don't have a lightbox, you can tape your pattern and fabric to a sunny window or patio door.

Personalizing Your Quilts with Lettering

Once you've decided to add lettering to your quilt, where do you begin? Examples of lettering styles (fonts) can be found in copyright-free publications, and font licenses (the right to use the font) can be purchased online. The word processing program in your personal computer probably has dozens of fonts. Inexpensive computer discs containing hundreds of fonts are readily available at your local office supply or discount store. Some of my favorite sources for fonts can be found on page 77.

Any project you create with your fonts may be used for your own enjoyment. However, if you wish to reproduce your lettering on an item for sale, be sure you have the appropriate font license.

I have provided complete alphabets for the six fonts used for the projects in this book. You can use a scanner or photocopier to enlarge the letters to any size you'd like. The alphabets can be found beginning on page 71.

To choose the best font for your project, you'll need to consider two main issues: style and ease of use.

Style

You want the style of your font to be compatible with the mood of your quilt. For an elegant, traditional quilt, you might consider a graceful Victorian font like the one used in *Home and Family* (page 24). If your quilt is bright with colorful, fun fabrics, a bold and graphic font like the one used in *Hugs & Kisses* (page 60) would be your best bet.

Detail *Home and Family*

Detail *Hugs & Kisses*

Some fonts evoke the feeling of a particular time or place. The font I used in *La Vie en Rose* (page 54), which is called Parisian, was the perfect choice to complement my Eiffel Tower border fabric.

Detail *La Vie en Rose*

Ease of Use

When selecting your font, choose a style that will be easy to read on the finished quilt and will not be too difficult to cut out and stitch. Letters with simple, thick shapes are the easiest to work with.

When using your computer's word processing program, you can easily alter the size of the font (point size) to fit your project. Sometimes a complex-looking letter becomes easy enough to work with when enlarged. Take some time to play with different letter styles and see how they look when enlarged.

Lettering Techniques

Adapting Letters for Appliqué

I love old-fashioned fonts. The lettering styles from the past have such style and grace. Unfortunately for quilt-makers, these fonts are sometimes not suited for appliqué, but here are some tips and techniques that will help you use them successfully.

The font I used in *Nest Pillow* (page 18) is an old-fashioned-style script. The original letters had some thin areas that would have been quite challenging to work with, but fattening up the thinnest sections makes the letters much easier to appliqué. Simply trace the original letter onto tracing paper and adjust it where needed. Try to make your size increases consistent from letter to letter.

Original letters

Fattening up the letters

Adding a Shadow with Contrasting Fabric

Some of the most interesting fonts have shadow lines that make the letters look three-dimensional. For medium to large letters, you can replicate this effect by using two different fabrics: one for the letter and the other for the shadow. The easiest way to do this is to trace and cut out two of each letter and place them on your background fabric, overlapping them until you get the look you want. Adding shadows is also an easy way to introduce another color into your project. See the seasonal table runners (page 37) for examples of this technique.

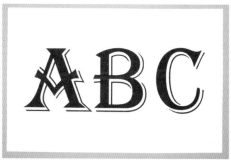

Original letters

Two fabrics for each letter

Finished letters

Adding a Shadow with Embroidered Details

If your letters are small, appliquéing the shadow lines may not be feasible. You can still get a shadow effect by tracing lines where the shadows would be and hand embroidering the lines using embroidery floss in a matching or contrasting color and an outline stitch. Instructions for the outline stitch are on page 14. I used this method on *Happily Ever After* (page 42).

Original letters

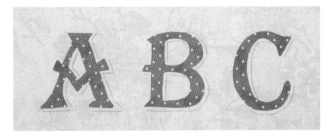

Ready for appliqué and embroidery

Finished letters

Combining Appliqué and Embroidery

The addition of simple outline-stitch embroidery can often make a font with delicate lines usable. An example of this technique can be seen in *La Vie en Rose* (page 54). The letters can be divided into segments, with only the thickest areas appliquéd. To complete the letter, use embroidery floss in a color that matches the appliqué, and outline stitch the traced lines. Instructions for the outline stitch are on page 14.

Original letters

Ready for appliqué and embroidery

Finished letters

Embroidery Only

Part of the beauty of script lettering is the delicate shapes of each letter and the flowing tails that connect the letters as they form words. Outline-stitch embroidery (page 14) is perfect for stitching such letters.

General Quiltmaking Instructions

Fusible Web Appliqué

1. Draw or trace your letters or motifs onto paper. Be aware that you will need to trace the reverse side onto the fusible web.

2. Trace the reverse side of each shape onto the paper side of the fusible web using a permanent marker, leaving ½″ between shapes. (Note that the letters and appliqué patterns from the projects in this book have already been reversed for you.) Trace each letter or motif onto the fusible web the number of times you will use it.

Note: If you are using a product, such as Lite Steam-A-Seam 2, that has paper on both sides, trace onto the side that is most firmly adhered to the adhesive material.

3. Cut out the motifs, leaving ¼″ around each one.

Motifs traced on fusible web

Motifs cut and ready for fusing

4. Following the manufacturer's instructions, press each appliqué motif to the wrong side of your chosen fabric and cut out directly on the drawn line.

Appliqué motifs fused onto fabrics

Appliqué motifs ready to be fused onto background fabric

5. Peel off the paper backing and, following the manufacturer's instructions, fuse each appliqué piece onto the background fabric.

Peel off paper backing.

Fuse appliqué motif in place.

Note: In some projects, such as *Nest Pillow* (page 18), some appliqué shapes will overlap others. The pattern pieces indicate which shapes overlap each other.

Machine Blanket Stitching

Before stitching directly on your project, sew a sample to check your machine's tension and stitch settings. The blanket stitch should look smooth and should have no bobbin "pop-ups." If the bobbin thread shows, your top tension is too tight. If the upper thread shows on the back, your bobbin tension is too tight. I like my blanket stitches to be about $\frac{1}{8}''$ long and $\frac{1}{8}''$ apart.

1. Place your fabric under the presser foot so the needle enters exactly at the edge of the appliqué piece. With the machine set on a regular straight stitch, insert the needle into the fabric to take a stitch and pull the bobbin thread up from the back. Holding both thread ends, make several tiny straight stitches to lock the threads.

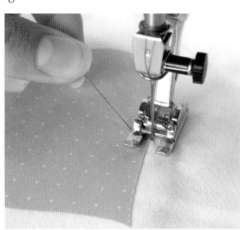

Beginning position

2. Switch to the blanket stitch. The blanket stitch consists of two parts: a straight stitch that moves your work forward and a horizontal stitch that "bites" the appliqué piece. Many machines bite on the left, but some bite on the right, so familiarize yourself with your machine before you begin.

3. Be sure the needle is exactly on the edge of the appliqué piece when you begin to stitch.

Proper needle placement

4. Stitch around each appliqué piece, slowing down as necessary to maintain control around inner and outer corners.

Maintaining control around curved shapes

5. When you reach the starting point, end with a few more tiny straight stitches and clip the threads.

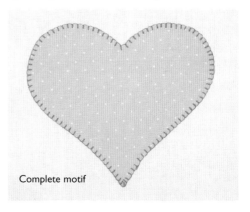

Complete motif

Blanket Stitching Around Inner and Outer Corners

Your stitching will look best if the bite stitches are placed so as to evenly divide inner and outer corners. If you keep your stitches small, it's easy to fudge a little to stitch perfect corners.

1. Slow down as you approach the inner or outer corner. When you are a straight stitch away, stop with the needle up, lift the presser foot, and adjust the fabric as necessary, so that the next straight stitch will end exactly at the corner point.

Straight stitch at corner

2. Pivot the fabric so that the bite stitch will divide the angle of the corner in half. Lower the presser foot and stitch the bite stitch. Pivot the fabric again to resume stitching.

Stitching around inner corner

Outline-Stitch Embroidery

For consistent tension on your stitching, an embroidery hoop is a must.

1. Cut off about 18″ of floss from the skein. The floss has 6 strands, but you will be using only 2 at a time. Separate one strand at a time from your 18″ length and put 2 strands together. Tie a small knot at the end of your length of floss.

2. Work from left to right, always keeping your thread to the left of the needle. To begin, pull the needle and floss up from the back of the fabric. To make the first stitch, insert the needle about 1/8″ away from the starting point. Bring the needle back up through the fabric at a point halfway from where you started your stitch. Pull the thread taut.

Outline stitch detail:
first stitch

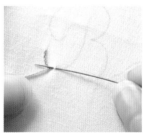

Outline stitch detail

3. For each subsequent stitch, insert the needle about 1/8″ away and bring the needle back up where your last stitch went in, following your marked stitching line.

Do not let your thread travel more than about 1/4″ across the back of your work. To get to a new starting point it's better to run your thread under a few stitches on the back. End the line of stitching with a knot on the back of the work.

Piecing

It is important to use an accurate $\frac{1}{4}''$ seam allowance when piecing. Set your stitch length to about 12 stitches per inch (2.0–2.5mm).

Careful pinning will improve your accuracy, as will the use of good pins. Treat yourself to a new package of extra-fine glass-head pins—they're worth every penny.

When piecing the borders, cut the border strips to the size of your quilt top, measured across the center; this measurement may be slightly larger or smaller than the measurements specified in the project instructions.

Pressing

Press all seams carefully in one direction, as indicated in the project instructions. Press from the right side of the work so you can avoid pressing in tucks. I like to use lots of steam when pressing. Avoid moving the iron back and forth over the fabric, which can cause distortion.

Layering

Place the backing (pieced, if necessary) wrong side up on a table or the floor. The backing can be taped onto a table or other hard surface or pinned to a carpeted floor. Make sure the backing is smooth. Place the batting on top of the backing and trim the batting slightly smaller than the backing. Carefully center the quilt top on the batting, right side up, and smooth out any wrinkles.

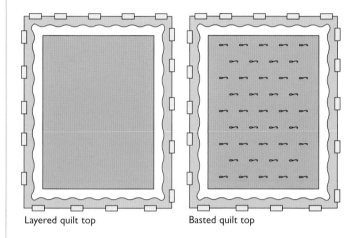

Layered quilt top   Basted quilt top

Basting

To baste a quilt for machine quilting, use very small brass safety pins. Start at the center of the quilt and work outward, placing a safety pin every 3″ and continuing to smooth the quilt top as you go.

Quilting

I like to have the appliqué in my quilts take center stage, so simple, traditional quilting works best for me. I generally quilt in the ditch around the lettering and other motifs, which gives the shapes more dimension. For background quilting, I prefer grids or allover designs that don't detract from the appliqué. When deciding on a border design, keep the style of the quilt in mind. For my vintage-style designs, I like traditional cables, feathers, or swags, which add softness and complement the curving lines in the letters.

Binding

1. Trim the batting and backing even with the quilt top.

2. Cut 2¼″ strips across the width of the binding fabric, as indicated in the project instructions. Using diagonal seams, piece the strips together to form one long strip.

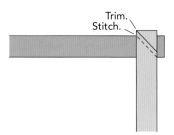

Sew diagonal seams.

3. Trim the seam allowances and press the seams open.

Trim and press.

4. Fold the binding in half lengthwise, wrong sides together, and press well. Keeping raw edges even, pin the binding strip to one edge of the quilt, beginning a few inches from a corner. Leaving the first few inches of the binding strip free, begin sewing with a ¼″ seam allowance. Stop ¼″ away from the first corner and backstitch.

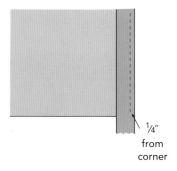

¼″ from corner

Stitch binding to first side of quilt top.

5. Remove the quilt from the machine. Pivot the quilt and fold the binding up so that it forms a straight line extending above the quilt.

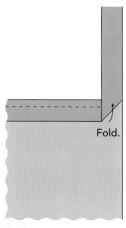

Fold.

Fold up.

6. Fold the binding down, keeping the fold even with the top edge of the quilt. Begin sewing at the folded edge and continue until you are ¼″ away from the next corner; backstitch.

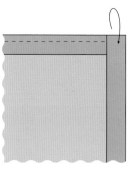

Fold down.

7. Repeat Steps 5 and 6 until you are about 6″ away from where you started. Remove the quilt from the sewing machine. To join the binding ends, fold the end binding strip back on itself so that the fold meets the beginning binding strip. Cut the folded binding tail 2¼″ from the fold.

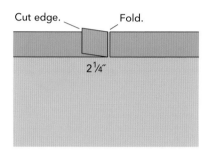

Binding trimmed for finishing

8. Open both tails and place one tail on top of the other, right sides together and at right angles. Stitch a diagonal seam, trim the seam allowance to ¼″, and press the seam open.

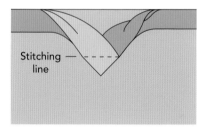

Binding seam

9. Finish sewing the binding to the quilt.

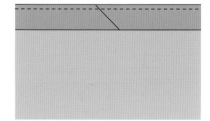

Binding stitching completed

10. Turn the folded edge of the binding to the back of the quilt and slipstitch in place by hand.

Label

Your quilt isn't truly complete until you have sewn a label onto it, providing the recipient (not to mention future generations) with your name, date, and any other pertinent information. I like to design and make a special label for each quilt before I have completed it. That way I can sew the label on when I'm slipstitching my binding.

Quilt label

Joy Pillow and Nest Pillow

The easy-to-make *Joy Pillow* doesn't have to be for Christmas only. Feel free to choose prints in your favorite colors to add joy to your home all year long.
To celebrate spring, make the *Nest Pillow* to grace your favorite chair.

Pillow size: 18″ × 18″
Lettering Technique: Adapting Letters for Appliqué

Fabric Requirements

Fabric amounts are based on 40″ fabric width.

For *Joy Pillow:*

- Aqua and white small-scale print for appliqué background, corner squares, and upper pillow back: ¾ yard
- Aqua and red large-scale floral print for setting triangles and lower pillow back: ¾ yard
- Red with white dots for letters and button covers: ¼ yard
- Aqua, red, and green small-scale print for border: ¼ yard
- Fusible web: ¼ yard
- Red stripe for binding: ⅓ yard

For *Nest Pillow:*

- Off-white and tan stripe for appliqué background and corner squares: 1 fat quarter or ½ yard
- Blue and pink floral print for setting triangles: ⅓ yard
- Scraps of brown, tan, green, blue, pink, and yellow prints for nest, branches, leaves, eggs, blossom, and blossom center
- Blue and pink paisley for border: ¼ yard
- Scrap of off-white print to cover buttons
- Red/pink tone-on-tone print for letters and binding: ⅓ yard
- Fusible web: ⅓ yard
- Blue and pink small-scale floral for upper pillow back: ⅝ yard
- Blue and pink medium-scale floral for lower pillow back: ⅝ yard

Also Required (for each pillow):

- Muslin for pillow top backing: 20″ × 20″
- Cotton batting: 20″ × 20″
- 1⅛″ half-ball covered buttons for pillow back: 3
- Pillow form: 18″ × 18″

Cutting

- Appliqué background and corner squares: Cut one square 10½″ × 10½″. Cut 4 squares 2½″ × 2½″.
- Setting triangles: Cut 2 squares 8½″ × 8½″; then cut each in half diagonally to make 4 triangles.
- Border: Cut 2 strips 2½″ × width of fabric; then cut into 4 strips 14½″ long.
- Upper pillow back: Cut one square 18″ × 18″.
- Lower pillow back: Cut one rectangle 18″ × 24″.
- Binding: Cut 3 strips 2¼″ × width of fabric.

Piecing

Use ¼″ seam allowances. Press seams in the directions indicated by the arrows.

1. Measure and mark the center on each side of the appliqué background square and on the longest side of each setting triangle. Match the center markings and stitch the triangles to opposite sides of the appliqué background square. Press.

2. Repeat for the remaining sides of the square.

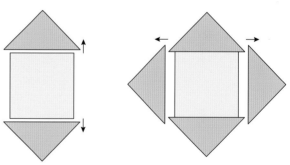

Stitch triangles to square.

3. Trim to measure 14½″ × 14½″. Be sure to leave a ¼″ seam allowance beyond the corners of the appliqué background square.

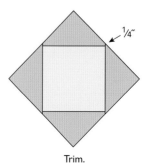

Trim.

4. Stitch a 14½″ border strip to each side of the pillow top. Press toward the borders. Stitch a corner square to each end of the remaining 2 border strips. Press away from the squares. Stitch these border units to the top and bottom of the pillow top. Press toward the borders. Your pillow top should now measure 18½″ × 18½″.

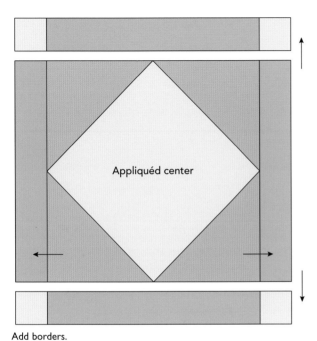

Add borders.

Appliqué

For *Joy Pillow:*

Prepare the letters for appliqué following the instructions on page 12. Fuse and blanket-stitch appliqué the letters in place, following the instructions on (pages 12–14).

For *Nest Pillow:*

Prepare the letters and the nest and branch pieces for appliqué following the instructions on page 12. Arrange the pieces on the background square, paying attention to pieces that are overlapped by others (shown with dotted lines on the patterns). Fuse and blanket-stitch appliqué all the pieces in place, following the instructions on pages 12–14.

Quilting and Finishing

1. Layer and baste the pillow top to the muslin square and quilt.

2. Trim the pillow top to measure 18″ × 18″.

> **Tip** Your pillow top will finish slightly smaller than the pillow form, which allows the pillow form to fit more snugly and attractively.

3. Fold the upper pillow back in half, wrong sides together, to measure 18″ × 9″. Press. Mark and sew 3 vertical 1⅛″ buttonholes on the folded edge through both layers of fabric. Two of the buttonholes should be placed 4¼″ from each side, and the remaining buttonhole should be placed at the center point, 9″ from the sides. The buttonholes should finish 1″ from the fold.

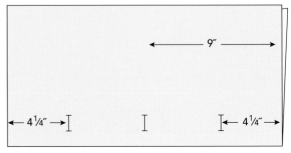

Buttonhole guide

4. Fold the lower pillow back in half, wrong sides together, to measure 18″ × 12″. Press. Overlap the upper pillow back over the lower pillow back so that the entire back measures 18″ × 18″. Following the manufacturer's instructions, cover the buttons with fabric. Mark button placement on the lower pillow back and sew the buttons in place. Button the upper pillow back to the lower pillow back.

5. Pin the pillow back to the pillow front, wrong sides together, and hand baste along the outside edges.

6. Following the instructions on pages 16–17, prepare and stitch 3 strips of binding to the pillow top. Remove the basting.

7. Insert the pillow form.

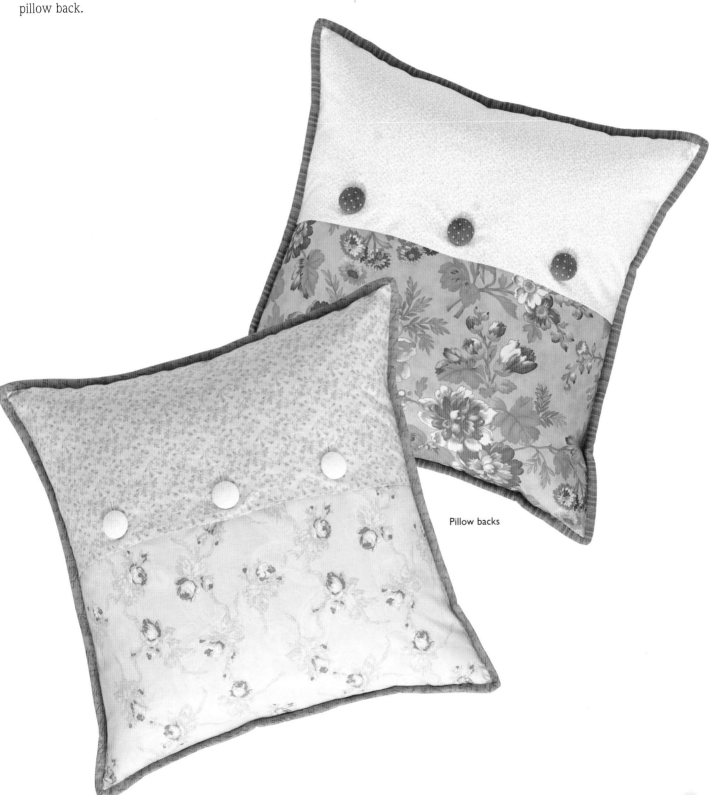

Pillow backs

Cut 1.

Cut 1.

Cut 1.

Cut 1.

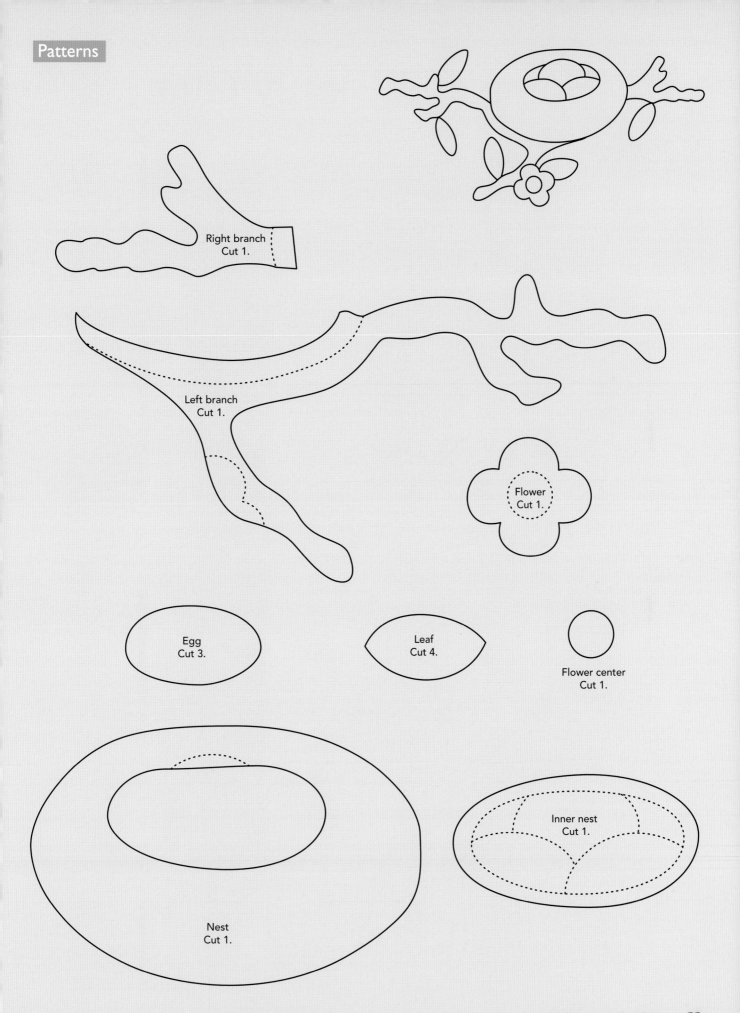

Right branch
Cut 1.

Left branch
Cut 1.

Flower
Cut 1.

Egg
Cut 3.

Leaf
Cut 4.

Flower center
Cut 1.

Nest
Cut 1.

Inner nest
Cut 1.

Home and Family Quilt

With its Flying Birds blocks, this quilt provides places for loved ones to add their signatures, making the project perfect to commemorate a family reunion or an anniversary.

Quilt size: $56\frac{1}{2}'' \times 65\frac{1}{2}''$
Finished block size: 9″
Lettering Technique: Adapting Letters for Appliqué

Fabric Requirements

Fabric amounts are based on 40″ fabric width.

- Assorted light to medium prints in creams, tans, and pinks for blocks: 1¾ yards total
- Assorted medium to dark prints in pinks, tans, blue, and red for blocks: 1 yard total
- Dark red tone-on-tone print for letters: ¾ yard
- Scraps of blue, pink, and red prints for corner appliqué motifs
- Rosy red print for inner border: ⅓ yard
- Tan tone-on-tone print for outer border (cut lengthwise): 1¾ yards
- Fusible web: 1½ yard
- Cotton batting: 60″ × 69″
- Backing (pieced widthwise): 3½ yards
- Binding: ⅝ yard

Cutting

- From assorted light to medium prints: Cut a total of 10 squares 9⅞″ × 9⅞″; then cut each in half diagonally. Cut 20 sets of 2 matching squares 3⅞″ × 3⅞″; then cut in half diagonally to form 3 half-square triangles (you will have one triangle left over).
- From assorted medium to dark prints: Cut 20 sets of 3 matching squares 3⅞″ × 3⅞″; then cut in half diagonally to form 6 half-square triangles.
- From rosy red print: Cut 5 strips 1½″ wide × width of fabric. Join the strips with diagonal seams to make one long strip. Press seams open. From this piece, cut 2 strips 45½″ long and 2 strips 38½″ long.
- From tan tone-on-tone print: Cut 4 lengthwise strips 9½″ wide × 60″ long.
- From binding fabric: Cut 7 strips 2¼″ × width of fabric.

Piecing

Use ¼″ seam allowances. Press seams in the directions indicated by the arrows.

1. To make each Flying Birds block, stitch 3 light-medium half-square triangles to 3 medium-dark half-square triangles to form 3 half-square triangle units.

Make 3 half-square triangle units.

2. Stitch 2 half-square triangle units together.

3. Add a dark triangle.

4. Add a dark triangle to the remaining half-square triangle unit.

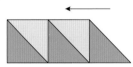

5. Sew the units into rows.

6. Add a large light-medium triangle. Your block should now measure 9½″ × 9½″. Repeat to make a total of 20 Flying Birds blocks.

7. Place the blocks in a pleasing arrangement that is 4 blocks wide and 5 blocks long.

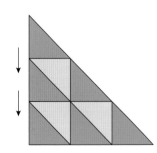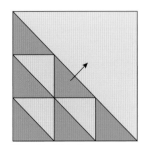

Completed block

8. Stitch the blocks into rows. Press the seams in alternate directions. Stitch the rows together and press each seam downward. Your quilt top should now measure 36½″ × 45½″.

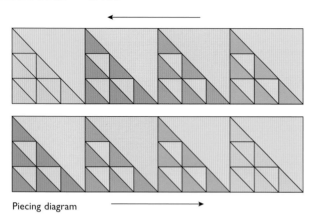

Piecing diagram

9. Stitch a 45½″ inner-border strip to each side of the quilt top. Press toward the inner borders. Stitch a 38½″ inner-border strip to the top and bottom of the quilt top. Press toward the inner borders.

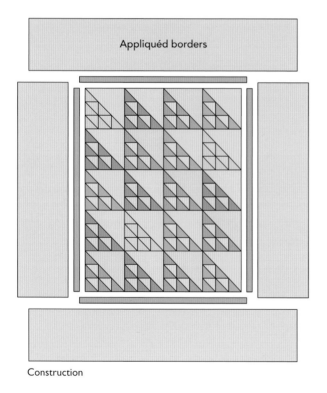

Construction

Outer-Border Appliqué

It is much easier to appliqué the letters to the outer-border strips before stitching the strips to your quilt top. The corner motifs, however, will need to be appliquéd after the outer borders have been stitched.

1. Using an erasable fabric pen, mark vertical lines 47½″ apart on 2 outer-border strips. These 2 strips will be stitched to the sides of your quilt top after the appliqué is complete.

2. Using an erasable fabric pen, mark vertical lines 56½″ apart on the remaining 2 outer-border strips. These strips will be stitched to the top and bottom of your quilt top after the appliqué is complete.

3. Using an erasable fabric pen, mark guidelines for letter placement 5½″ from the top of each outer-border strip. The bottom edges of the lowercase letters will be placed on that line. The top edges of the uppercase letters will be placed approximately 1¾″ from the top of each outer-border strip.

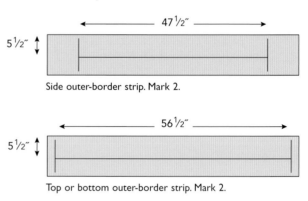

Side outer-border strip. Mark 2.

Top or bottom outer-border strip. Mark 2.

4. Prepare the letters and corner motifs for appliqué following the instructions on page 12.

5. Use the quilt photo as a guide for letter placement and for the spacing of the outer-border strips for the top and both sides. For the bottom outer-border strip, the spacing is determined by the number of letters in the family name you are using.

6. Fuse and blanket-stitch appliqué the letters in place, following the instructions on pages 12–14.

7. Cut the border strips to the marked length. Stitch the side outer-border strips to the quilt top. Press toward the inner borders. Stitch the top and bottom outer-border strips to the quilt top. Press toward the inner borders.

8. Fuse and blanket-stitch appliqué the corner motifs in place.

Quilting and Finishing

1. Layer, baste, and quilt your quilt top.

2. Following the instructions on pages 16–17, prepare and stitch 7 binding strips, or use leftover fabric to make a scrappy binding, as I did.

Cut 4.

Cut 4.

Cut 12.

Cut 4.

Cut 4.

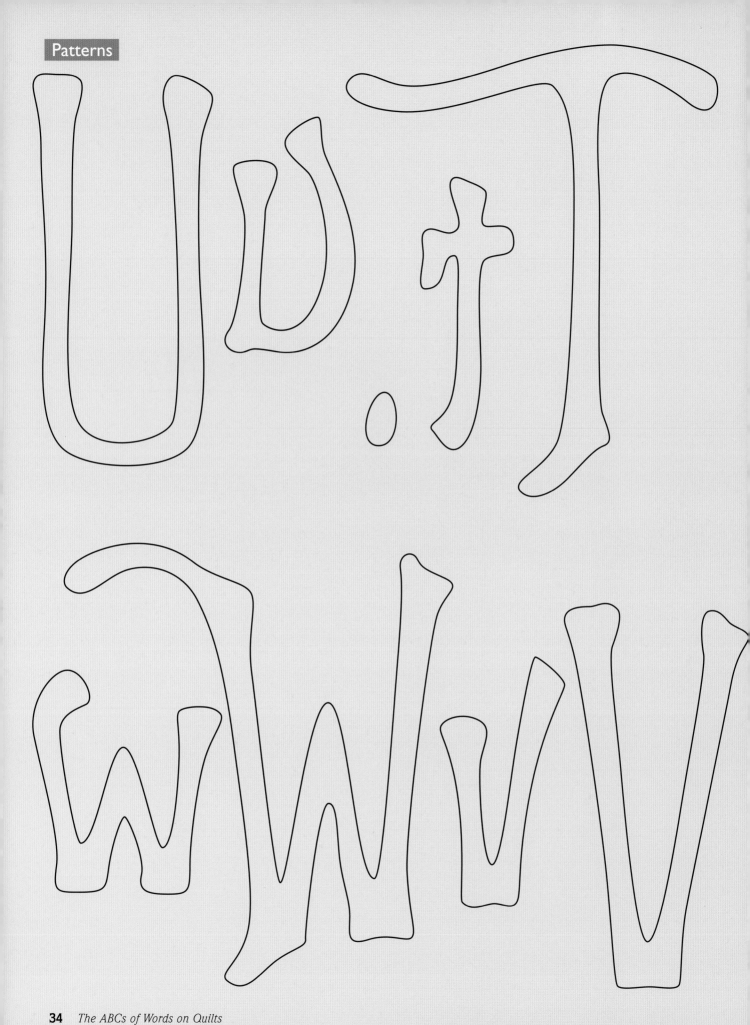

Seasonal Table Runners

Pieced and appliquéd by Elizabeth Scott; quilted by Pam Vieira-McGinnis

Table runner size: 39″ × 18½″
Lettering Technique: Adding a Shadow with Contrasting Fabric

Fabric Requirements

Fabric amounts are based on 40″ fabric width.

For each runner:

- Light-color tone-on-tone print for appliqué background: 1/3 yard
- Small-scale print or tone-on-tone print for letters: 1/4 yard each of 2 contrasting fabrics
- Contrasting tiny print for inner border: 1/8 yard
- Medium-scale print for outer border: 5/8 yard
- Fusible web: 5/8 yard
- Cotton batting: 22″ × 43″
- Backing: 2/3 yard
- Coordinating print for binding: 1/3 yard

Cutting

- From light-color tone-on-tone print: Cut one rectangle 10″ × 31″. This piece will be trimmed after appliqué is complete.
- From contrasting tiny print: Cut 2 strips 1″ × width of fabric; then cut into 2 strips 29″ long and 2 strips 9½″ long.
- From medium-scale print: Cut 3 strips 5″ × width of fabric; then cut into 2 strips 30″ long and 2 strips 18½″ long.
- From coordinating print: Cut 3 strips 2¼″ × width of fabric.

Appliqué

1. Prepare the letters for appliqué following the directions on page 12. You may find it easier to position your letters by drawing a guideline 3/4″ from the top of the appliqué background piece using an erasable fabric pen. The tops of most letters can be placed along the marked line.

 You can use this method to add shadows to many styles of block letters.

 With some letters you will have very narrow shadow lines, so it's easier to stitch the bottom (shadow) letters first and then fuse and stitch the upper letters.

2. Place both layers of the letters in position. Remove the upper letters. Fuse and blanket-stitch appliqué the shadow letters, following the instructions on pages 12–14. Place the upper letters back in position. Fuse and blanket-stitch appliqué the upper letters.

3. Trim the appliquéd background rectangle to measure 8½″ × 29″.

Piecing

Use 1/4″ seam allowances. Press seams in the directions indicated by the arrows.

1. Stitch a 29″ inner-border strip to the top and bottom of the appliquéd background piece. Press toward the inner borders. Stitch a 9½″ inner-border strip to each side. Press toward the inner borders.

2. Stitch a 30″ outer-border strip to the top and bottom of the runner. Press toward the inner borders. Stitch an 18½″ outer-border strip to each side of the runner. Press toward the inner borders.

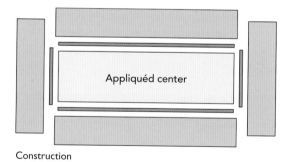

Appliquéd center

Construction

Quilting and Finishing

1. Layer, baste, and quilt your runner.

2. Following the instructions on pages 16–17, prepare and stitch 3 strips of binding to the runner.

Happily Ever After Quilt

Celebrate a wedding or an anniversary with a bridal bouquet wallhanging
featuring the bride's and groom's names and special date.

Quilt size: 30″ × 36″
Lettering Technique: Adding a Shadow with Embroidered Details

Fabric Requirements

Fabric amounts are based on 40″ fabric width.

- Tan tone-on-tone print for appliqué background (cut widthwise): 2/3 yard
- Assorted light green prints for leaves: 1/8 yard total
- Assorted cream, white, and pale pink prints for roses: 1/4 yard total
- White tone-on-tone print for letters: 1/4 yard
- Medium-scale cream and pink floral for bouquet ribbon: 1/8 yard
- Pale green and white floral for inner border and some leaves: 1/4 yard
- Cream and tan medium-scale print for outer border: 7/8 yard
- Fusible web: 3/4 yard
- Cotton batting: 34″ × 40″
- Backing (cut widthwise): 1 yard
- Tan and cream stripe for binding: 3/8 yard

Also Required:

- Embroidery floss in cream, light green, and pale pink
- Approximately 40 cream and white buttons ranging in size from 1/4″ to 1/2″ to embellish your bridal bouquet

Cutting

- From tan tone-on-tone print: Cut one rectangle 20″ × 26″. This piece will be trimmed after appliqué is complete.
- From pale green and white floral print: Cut 4 strips 1 1/4″ × width of fabric; then cut into 2 strips 20 1/2″ long and 2 strips 25″ long.
- From cream and tan medium-scale print: Cut 4 strips 5 1/4″ wide × width of fabric; then cut into 2 strips 26 1/2″ long and 2 strips 30″ long.
- From tan and cream stripe: Cut 4 strips 2 1/4″ × width of fabric.

Appliqué

1. Prepare the letters, flowers, leaves, and ribbon for appliqué following the instructions on page 12. When positioning the bouquet, pay attention to pieces that are overlapped by other pieces.

Appliqué guide

2. Fuse and blanket-stitch appliqué all the pieces in place, following the instructions on pages 12–14.

3. Draw the shadow lines on the words "Happily Ever After." Trace the letters and numbers needed for the names and date of your choice using the alphabet on page 76.

4. Following the instructions on page 14, embroider the shadow lines for the word "Happily" with light green floss, "Ever After" with pale pink floss, and the names and date with cream floss.

5. Trim the appliquéd background piece to measure 19″ × 25″.

To make the cream lettering show up against the tan background, add a second row of outline stitches next to the first.

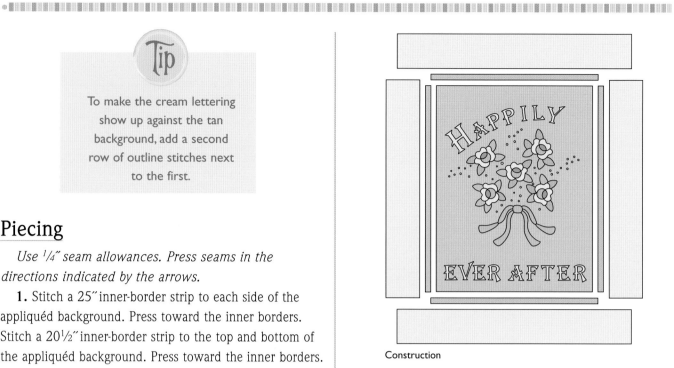

Construction

Piecing

Use ¼″ seam allowances. Press seams in the directions indicated by the arrows.

1. Stitch a 25″ inner-border strip to each side of the appliquéd background. Press toward the inner borders. Stitch a 20½″ inner-border strip to the top and bottom of the appliquéd background. Press toward the inner borders.

2. Stitch a 26½″ outer-border strip to each side of the quilt top. Press toward the inner borders. Stitch a 30″ outer-border strip to the top and bottom of the quilt top. Press toward the inner borders.

Quilting and Finishing

1. Layer, baste, and quilt your quilt top.

2. Following the instructions on pages 16–17, prepare and stitch 4 strips of binding to the quilt.

3. Hand stitch the buttons in place around the bouquet as shown on the appliqué guide (page 43).

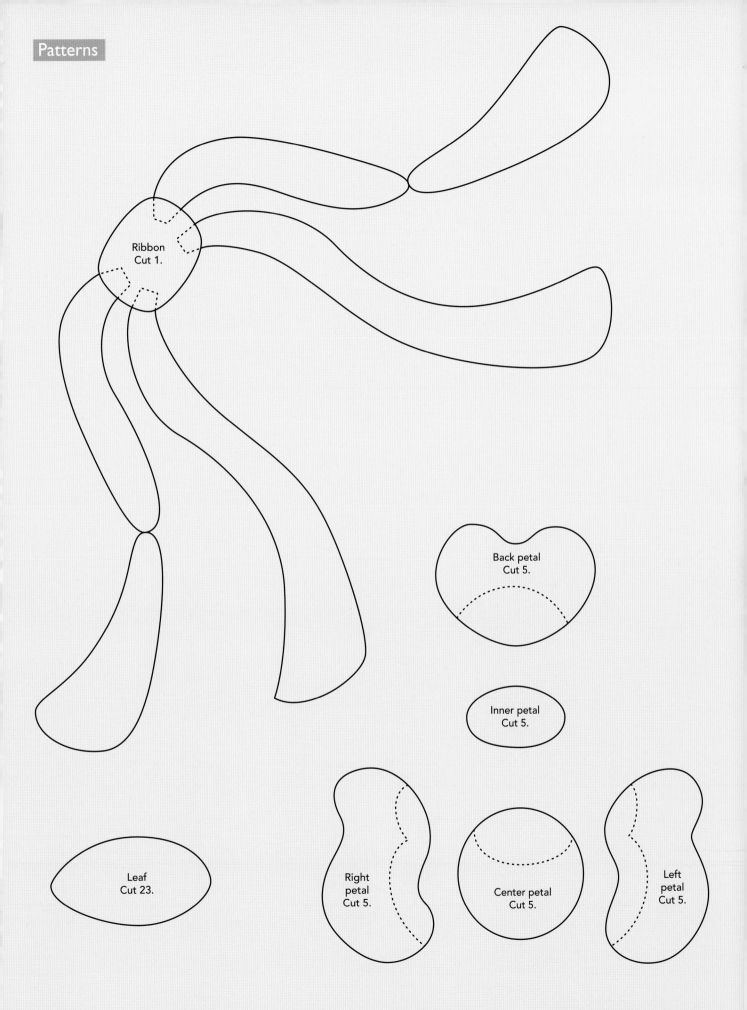

Ribbon
Cut 1.

Back petal
Cut 5.

Inner petal
Cut 5.

Leaf
Cut 23.

Right
petal
Cut 5.

Center petal
Cut 5.

Left
petal
Cut 5.

Cut 2. Cut 1. Cut 1.

Cut 1. Cut 1. Cut 1. Cut 2.

Cut 3. Cut 2. Cut 1. Cut 1.

Sweet Dreams Baby Quilt

For an extra-special project, embroider the baby's name
and choose fabrics that coordinate with the nursery.

Quilt size: $37\frac{1}{2}$" × $44\frac{1}{2}$"

Finished block size: $3\frac{1}{2}$"

Lettering Technique: Embroidery Only

Fabric Requirements

Fabric amounts are based on 40″ fabric width.

- Assorted pastel prints and plaids for blocks: 1¼ yards total
- Mottled light blue for birds and inner border: ½ yard
- White with pink dots for outer border: ⅝ yard
- Pink solid for banners and binding: ¾ yard
- White solid for banners: ⅓ yard
- Scrap of gold for beaks
- Fusible web: 1½ yards
- Cotton batting: 41″ × 48″
- Backing: 1⅜ yards

Also Required:

- Embroidery floss in blue, white, and charcoal gray

Cutting

- From assorted pastel prints and plaids: Cut 80 squares 4″ × 4″.
- From mottled light blue: Cut 4 strips 1½″ × width of fabric; then cut into 2 strips 30½″ long and 2 strips 35½″ long.
- From white with pink dots: Cut 4 strips 4″ × width of fabric; then cut into 4 strips 37½″ long.
- From pink solid: Cut 5 strips 2¼″ × width of fabric.

Piecing

Use ¼″ seam allowances. Press seams in the directions indicated by the arrows.

1. Place the assorted pastel squares in a pleasing arrangement that is 8 squares wide by 10 squares long.

2. Stitch the squares together into rows. Press the seams in alternate directions. Stitch the rows together and press the seams downward. Your quilt top should now measure 28½″ × 35½″.

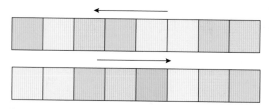

Piecing diagram

3. Stitch a 35½″ inner-border strip to each side of the quilt top. Press toward the inner borders. Stitch a 30½″ inner-border strip to the top and bottom of the quilt top. Press toward the inner borders.

4. Stitch a 37½″ outer-border strip to each side of the quilt top. Press toward the inner borders. Stitch a 37½″ outer-border strip to the top and bottom of the quilt top. Press toward the inner borders.

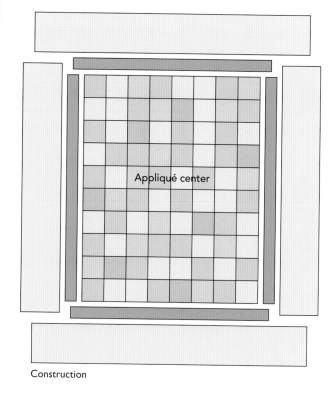

Construction

Embroidery and Appliqué

1. Trace the words "Sweet Dreams" and "Baby" (or the name of your choice, using the alphabet on page 72), onto the white solid fabric. Be sure to leave enough room around each one to cut out the banners. Embroider using 2 strands of blue embroidery floss and an outline stitch (page 14).

2. Trace the bird eyes onto a piece of mottled light blue fabric, making sure to leave enough room to trace and cut out the bird heads. Outline stitch the dark area of each eye and the eyelashes with 2 strands of charcoal gray embroidery floss. Fill in the dark area of each eye with straight stitches using 2 strands of charcoal gray embroidery floss. Use 2 strands of white floss to straight stitch highlights on each eye.

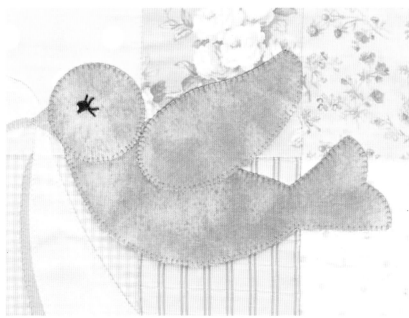

3. Prepare all the pieces for appliqué following the instructions on page 12. Be sure to center the embroidered words on the white banner pieces.

4. When positioning the bird heads, be sure to match the embroidered eyes to the eye placement lines on the appliqué pattern. Position the banner pieces with the pink banner starting about 1″ below the top of the white piece and extending approximately ¼″ beyond it.

5. Fuse and blanket-stitch appliqué all the pieces in place, following the instructions on pages 12–14.

Bird eye detail

Quilting and Finishing

1. Layer, baste, and quilt your quilt top.

2. Following instructions on pages 16–17, prepare and stitch 5 strips of binding to the quilt.

Banner detail

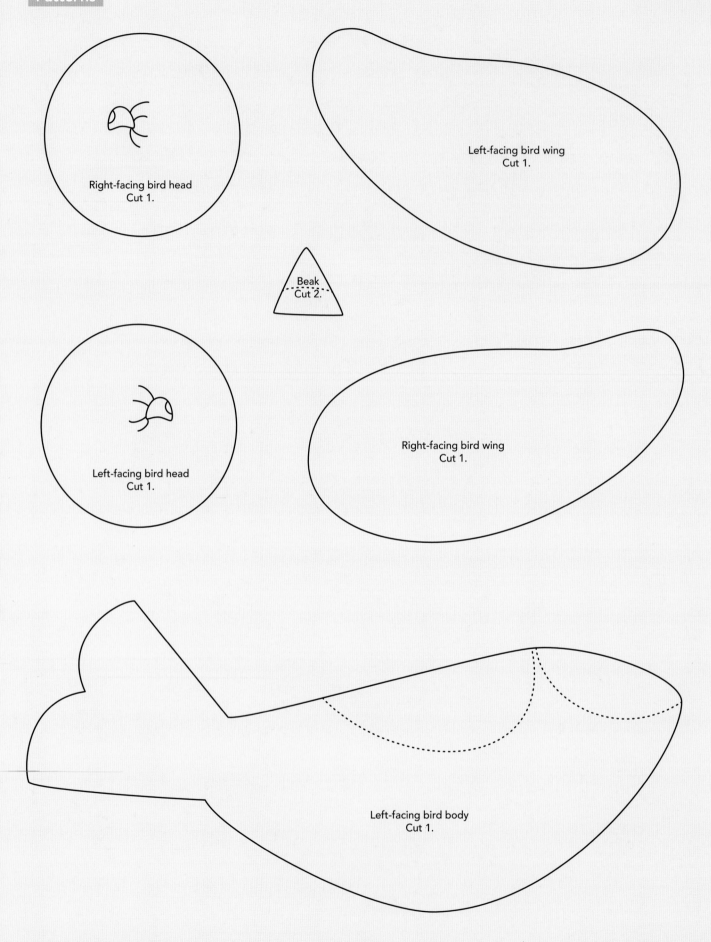

Right-facing bird head
Cut 1.

Left-facing bird wing
Cut 1.

Beak
Cut 2.

Left-facing bird head
Cut 1.

Right-facing bird wing
Cut 1.

Left-facing bird body
Cut 1.

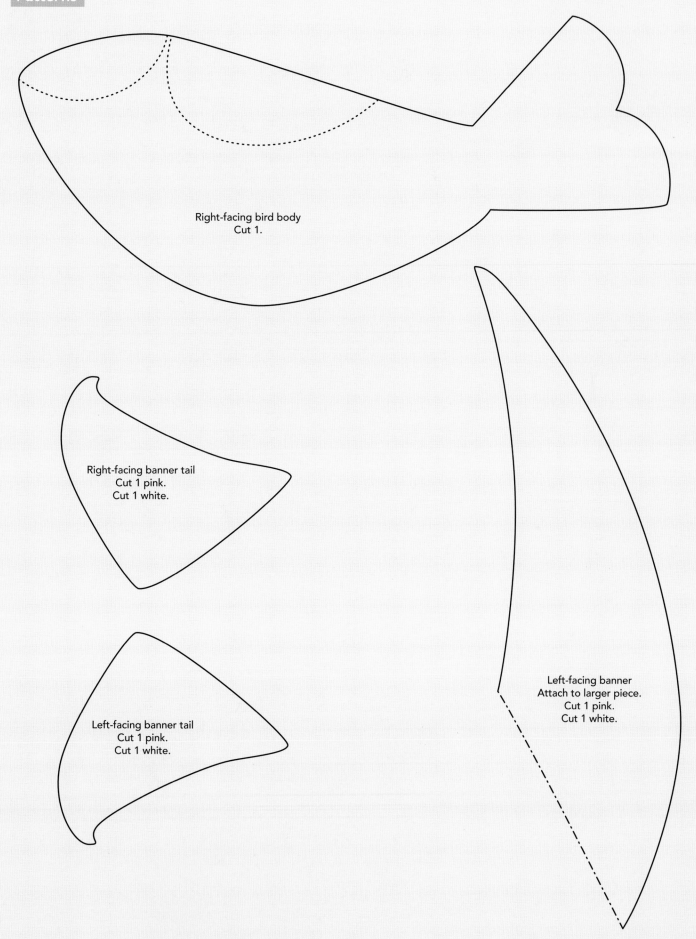

Right-facing bird body
Cut 1.

Right-facing banner tail
Cut 1 pink.
Cut 1 white.

Left-facing banner tail
Cut 1 pink.
Cut 1 white.

Left-facing banner
Attach to larger piece.
Cut 1 pink.
Cut 1 white.

Note: The lettering for "Sweet Dreams" is shown on the right-facing banner pattern piece so the letters would not be reversed. Use the left-facing pattern pieces for the banner.

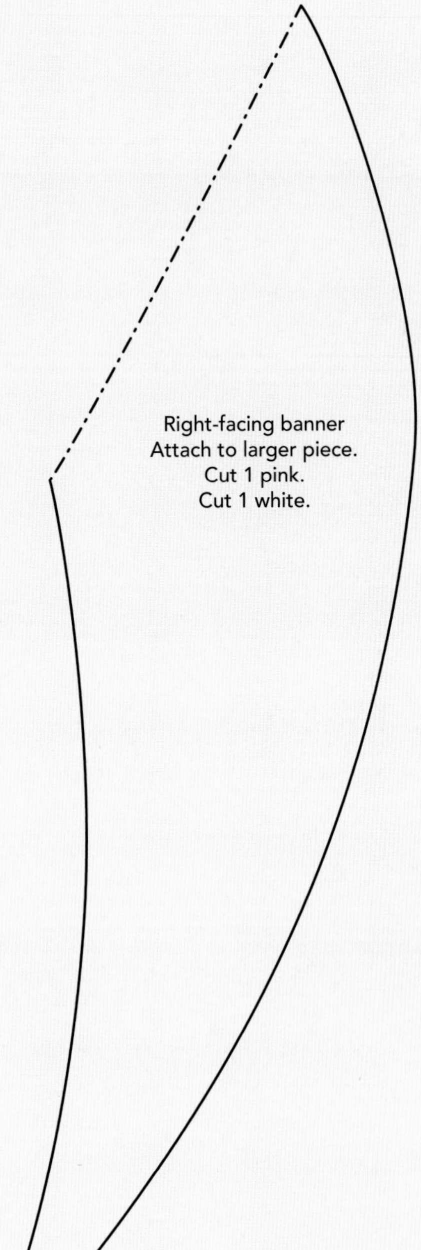

Right-facing banner
Cut 1 pink.
Cut 1 white.

Right-facing banner
Attach to larger piece.
Cut 1 pink.
Cut 1 white.

Dreams

Sweet

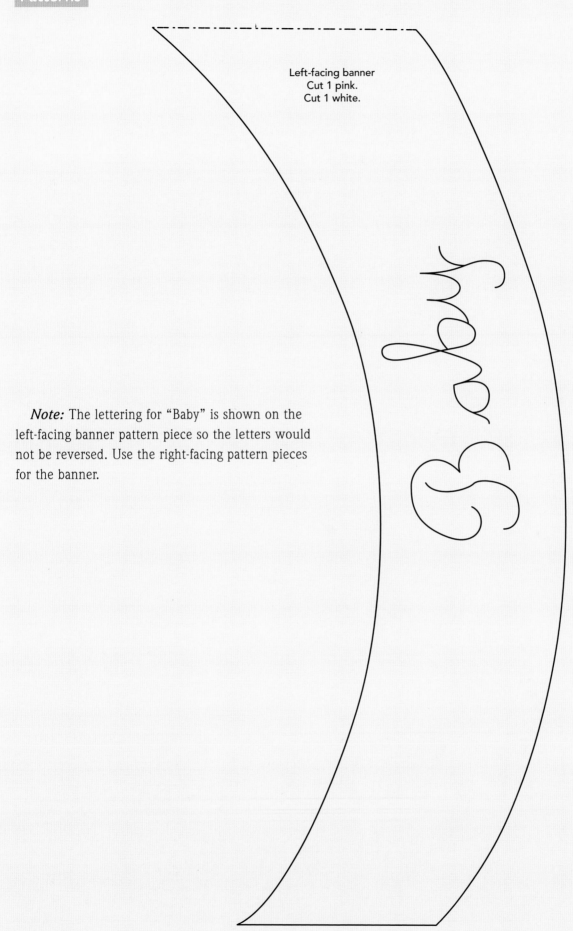

Left-facing banner
Cut 1 pink.
Cut 1 white.

Note: The lettering for "Baby" is shown on the left-facing banner pattern piece so the letters would not be reversed. Use the right-facing pattern pieces for the banner.

La Vie en Rose Quilt

Choose some bright, fun prints and celebrate the fact that life is rosy!

Quilt size: 33″ × 37″
Lettering Technique: Combining Appliqué and Embroidery

Fabric Requirements

Fabric amounts are based on 40″ fabric width.

- White with black dots for upper appliqué background: ½ yard
- Black-on-white print for lower appliqué background: ¼ yard
- White solid for appliquéd letters background: ⅓ yard
- Bright pink small-scale print for inner borders: ⅓ yard
- Assorted bright pink prints, black prints, and white prints for pieced border: ⅜ yard total
- Large-scale black print for outer border: ¾ yard (directional print: 1¼ yards)
- Black solid for letters: ⅛ yard
- Black print for vase: ¼ yard
- Assorted bright pinks for roses and blossoms: ¼ yard total
- Fusible web: ¾ yard
- Cotton batting: 37″ × 41″
- Backing: 1¼ yards
- Bright pink stripe for binding: ⅜ yard

Also required:

- Black embroidery floss

Cutting

- From white with black dots: Cut one rectangle 18½″ × 14½″. This piece will be trimmed after appliqué is complete.
- From black-on-white print: Cut one rectangle 18½″ × 6½″. This piece will be trimmed after appliqué is complete.
- From white solid: Cut one rectangle 9″ × 21″. This piece will be trimmed after appliqué is complete.
- From bright pink small-scale print: Cut 7 strips 1″ × width of fabric. Cut into 2 strips 17½″ long, 2 strips 24½″ long, 2 strips 22½″ long, and 2 strips 27½″ long.
- From assorted prints: Cut 35 squares 2½″ × 2½″.
- From large-scale black print: Cut 4 strips 5¼″ × width of fabric; then cut into 2 strips 23½″ long and 2 strips

37″ long. (For a directional print, cut 2 lengthwise strips 5¼″ × 37″; then cut 2 widthwise strips 5¼″ × 23½″.)

- From bright pink stripe: Cut 4 strips 2¼″ × width of fabric.

Piecing and Appliqué

Use ¼″ seam allowances. Press seams in the directions indicated by the arrows.

1. Stitch the upper background rectangle to the lower background rectangle on the 18½″ edges.

2. Following the instructions on page 12, prepare the vase and rose pieces for appliqué. Position the pieces and fuse in place.

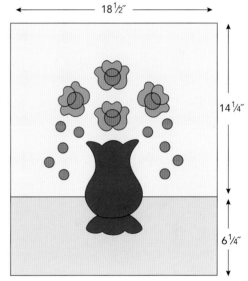

Pieced background

3. Lay the ¼-yard piece of white solid fabric over the words "La Vie en Rose." Position the appliqué segments in place and fuse. Trace the lines to be embroidered.

4. Blanket-stitch appliqué all the appliqué pieces, following the instructions on pages 13–14.

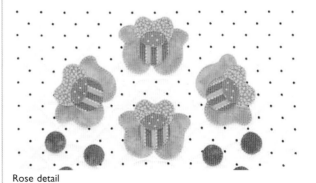

Rose detail

5. Following the instructions on page 14, embroider all the marked lines using 2 strands of black embroidery floss and an outline stitch. If desired, add a second row of outline stitching close to the first row to increase the thickness of the lines. Trim the lettering piece to measure 17½″ × 4½″.

6. Trim the sides of the appliquéd background piece to measure 17½″ wide. To trim the top and bottom to size, measure the lower rectangle 5¾″ from the seamline and cut. Measure the upper 13¾″ rectangle from the seamline and cut.

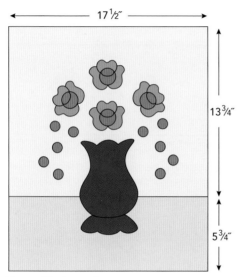

Trimmed background

7. Stitch a 17½″ inner-border strip to the top of the appliquéd background and to the top of the appliquéd lettering piece. Press toward the borders.

8. Stitch the appliquéd background piece to the lettering piece along the inner-border strip. Press toward the inner border.

9. Stitch a 24½″ inner-border strip to each side of the quilt top. Press toward the inner borders.

10. For each pieced side border, stitch a row of 12 assorted print squares. Press the seams downward. For the upper pieced border, stitch a row of 11 assorted print squares. Press the seams toward the left. Stitch a pieced border row to each side of the quilt top. Press toward the inner borders. Stitch the remaining pieced border row to the top edge. Press toward the inner borders.

11. Stitch a 22½″ inner-border strip to the top and bottom of the quilt top. Press toward the inner borders. Stitch a 27½″ inner-border strip to each side. Press toward the inner borders.

12. Stitch a 23½″ outer-border strip to the top and bottom of the quilt top. Press toward the inner borders. Stitch a 37″ outer-border strip to each side of the quilt top. Press toward the inner borders.

Construction

Quilting and Finishing

1. Layer, baste, and quilt your quilt top.

2. Following the instructions on pages 16–17, prepare and stitch 4 strips of binding to the quilt.

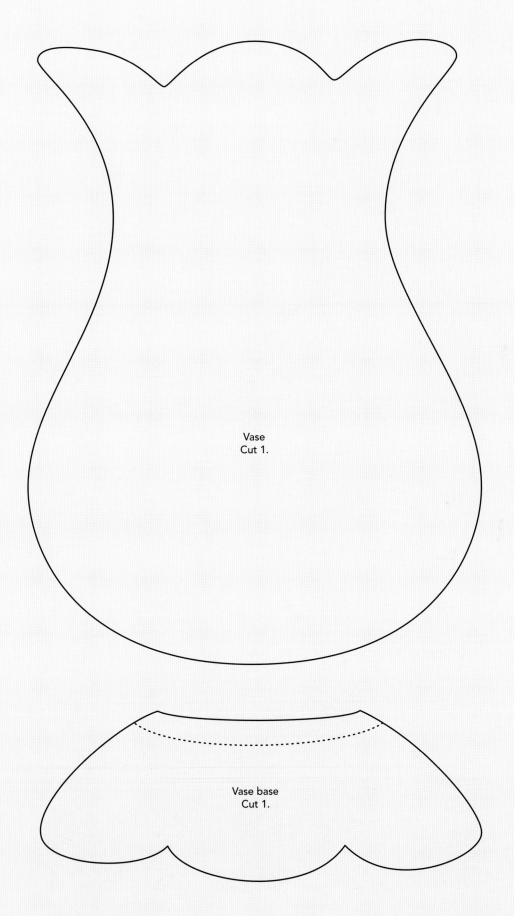

Vase
Cut 1.

Vase base
Cut 1.

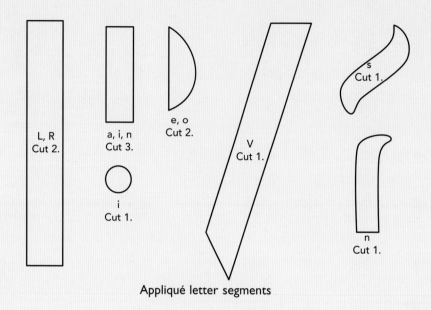

L, R
Cut 2.

a, i, n
Cut 3.

e, o
Cut 2.

i
Cut 1.

V
Cut 1.

s
Cut 1.

n
Cut 1.

Appliqué letter segments

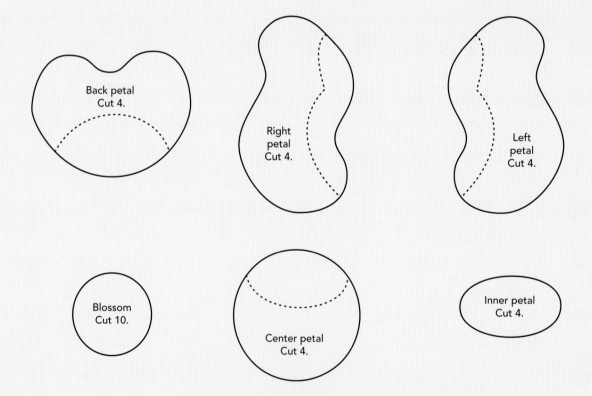

Back petal
Cut 4.

Right petal
Cut 4.

Left petal
Cut 4.

Blossom
Cut 10.

Center petal
Cut 4.

Inner petal
Cut 4.

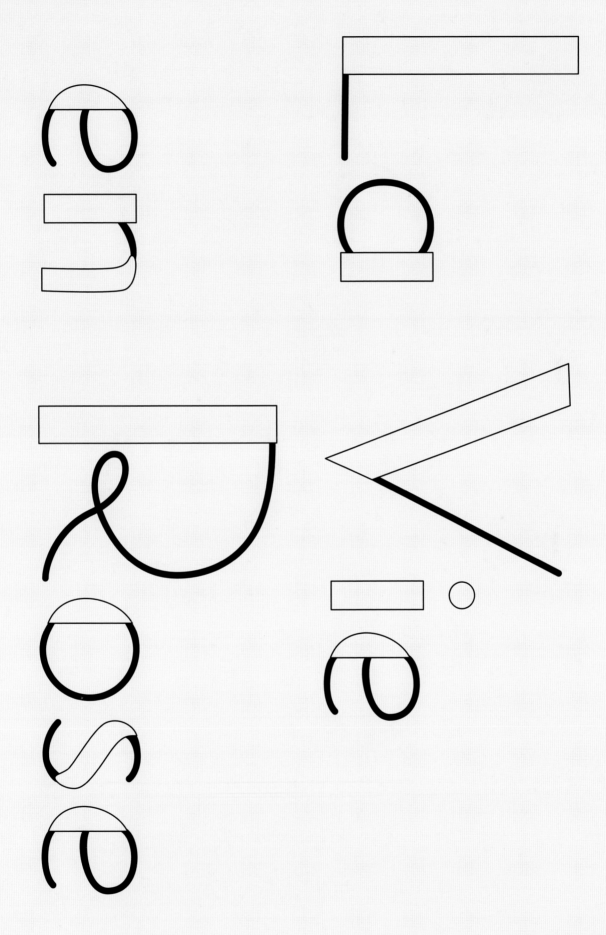

Hugs & Kisses Quilt

This sweet quilt uses block letters that are easy to appliqué. The informal placement
of motifs makes the project extra quick to make.

Quilt size: $38\frac{1}{2}'' \times 46\frac{1}{2}''$
Lettering Technique: Adapting Letters for Appliqué

Fabric Requirements

Fabric amounts are based on 40″ fabric width.

- Blue and white check for appliqué background (cut widthwise): ⅞ yard
- Assorted white background prints for sawtooth border: ½ yard total
- Assorted prints in red, pink, yellow, and green for sawtooth border and hearts: 1¼ yards total
- Pink and white dot for letters and binding: ⅝ yard
- Blue floral print for outer border: ⅞ yard
- Fusible web: 1½ yards
- Cotton batting: 42″ × 50″
- Backing: 1½ yards

Cutting

- From blue and white check: Cut one rectangle 25″ × 33″. This piece will be trimmed after appliqué is complete.
- From assorted white background prints: Cut 30 squares 2⅞″ × 2⅞″; then cut each in half diagonally to form 60 half-square triangles.
- From assorted red, pink, yellow, and green prints: Cut 30 squares 2⅞″ × 2⅞″; then cut each in half diagonally to form 60 half-square triangles.
- From blue floral print: Cut 4 strips 5½″ × width of fabric; then cut 2 strips 36½″ long and 2 strips 38½″ long.
- From pink and white dot: Cut 5 strips 2¼″ × width of fabric.

Appliqué

1. Prepare the letters and hearts for appliqué following the instructions on page 12.

2. Position the pieces randomly on the background.

3. Fuse and blanket-stitch appliqué all the pieces in place following the instructions on page 12–14.

 To make a light background print stand out, try using a contrasting color thread for the appliqué.

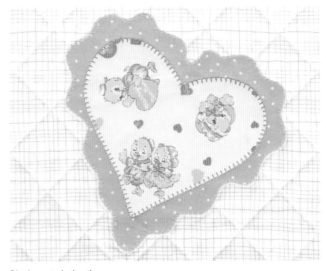

Blanket stitch detail

4. Trim the appliquéd background piece to measure 24½″ × 32½″.

Piecing

Use ¼″ seam allowances. Press seams in the directions indicated by the arrows.

1. Stitch each white print triangle to a colored print triangle to form half-square triangle units. Press toward the colored triangles. Make 60.

Half-square triangle unit

2. Stitch the half-square triangle units into rows. Make 2 rows of 16 units each and 2 rows of 14 units each. Note that the units change direction at the halfway point on each row. Press the seams in one direction.

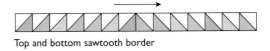

Top and bottom sawtooth border

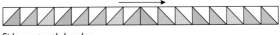

Side sawtooth border

3. Stitch a 16-unit row to each side of the appliquéd background, positioning each row so the colored triangles are toward the center of the quilt. Press toward the center. Stitch a 14-unit row to the top and bottom. Press toward the center.

4. Stitch a 36½″ outer-border strip to each side of the quilt top. Press toward the outer borders. Stitch a 38½″ outer-border strip to the top and bottom of the quilt. Press toward the outer borders.

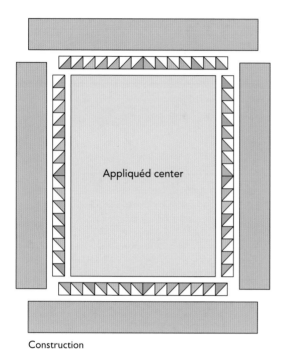

Construction

Quilting and Finishing

1. Layer, baste, and quilt your quilt top.

2. Following the instructions on pages 16–17, prepare and stitch 5 strips of binding to the quilt.

Cut 1.

Cut 1.

Cut 1.

Cut 1.

Cut 4.

Cut 1.

Cut 1.

Cut 1.

Medium heart
Cut 6.

Small heart
Cut 10.

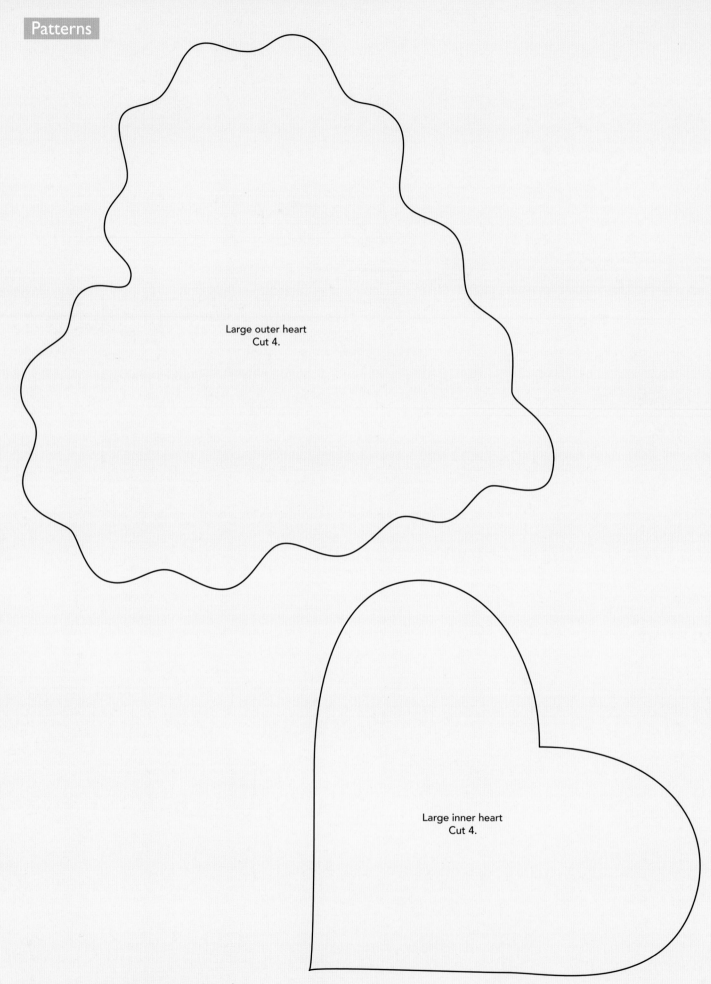

Large outer heart
Cut 4.

Large inner heart
Cut 4.

Garden Fresh Throw

Grab some summer-fresh prints and make a fun throw quilt
to take on your next picnic!

Quilt size: 60½″ × 60½″

Lettering Technique: Adapting Letters for Appliqué

Garden Fresh uses a retro-style cursive font. Letters like these can be
attached to each other to form one large appliqué piece. I curved the
word "Garden" to add some interest.

Fabric Requirements

Fabric amounts are based on 40″ fabric width.

- White solid for appliqué background in center and corners: $7/8$ yard

- Blue solid for letters and binding: $7/8$ yard

- Scraps of red, green, and brown prints for cherries, leaves, and stems

- Red pin dot for narrow borders and cherries: $5/8$ yard

- Large-scale blue floral print for wide inner border and piano key border: $3/4$ yard

- Assorted white background small-scale prints for Shoo-Fly blocks and piano key border: 1 yard total

- Assorted red and blue prints for Shoo-Fly blocks and piano key border: $3/4$ yard total

- Yellow and white check for squares for Shoo-Fly border: $5/8$ yard

- Additional assorted prints in red, yellow, and blue for piano key border: $1 3/8$ yards total

- Fusible web: $3/4$ yard

- Batting: 64″ × 64″

- Backing: $3 3/4$ yards

To make this quilt I added some pieces cut from retro-style print napkins and dishtowels. For a project like this, have fun with different fabrics.

Cutting

- From white solid: Cut one square $18 1/2″ × 18 1/2″$. Cut 4 squares $9 1/2″ × 9 1/2″$. These pieces will be trimmed after appliqué is complete.

- From red pin dot: Cut 10 strips $1 1/2″$ × width of fabric; then cut into 2 strips $17 1/2″$ long, 2 strips $19 1/2″$ long, 2 strips $28 1/2″$ long, and 2 strips $30 1/2″$ long. Join the remaining 4 strips with diagonal seams to make one long strip. Press the seams open. From this piece cut 2 strips $42 1/2″$ long and 2 strips $44 1/2″$ long.

- From large-scale blue floral print: Cut 3 strips $5″$ × width of fabric; then cut into 2 strips $19 1/2″$ long and 2 strips $28 1/2″$ long.

- From assorted white background small-scale prints: Cut 12 sets of 2 matching squares $2 7/8″ × 2 7/8″$; then cut each in half diagonally to form 4 half-square triangles. Cut 12 sets of 4 matching squares $2 1/2″ × 2 1/2″$.

- From assorted red and blue prints: Cut 12 sets of 2 matching squares $2 7/8″ × 2 7/8″$; then cut each in half diagonally to form 4 half-square triangles. From remaining fabric, cut 12 squares $2 1/2″ × 2 1/2″$.

- From yellow and white check: Cut 2 strips $6 1/2″$ × width of fabric; then cut into 12 squares $6 1/2″ × 6 1/2″$.

- From additional assorted prints and leftover blue floral, white background, and red and blue prints: Cut strips $2 1/2″$ wide × width of fabric; then cut into $2 1/2″ × 8 1/2″$ rectangles. You will need a total of 88 rectangles for the piano key border.

- From blue solid: Cut 7 strips $2 1/4″$ × width of fabric.

Appliqué

1. Prepare the letters, cherries, leaves, and stems for appliqué following the instructions on page 12. Center each bunch of cherries on the corner appliqué background pieces.

2. Fuse and blanket-stitch appliqué all the pieces in place following the instructions on pages 12–14.

Corner square detail

3. Trim the center appliquéd background piece to measure $17 1/2″ × 17 1/2″$. Trim the corner appliquéd background pieces to measure $8 1/2″ × 8 1/2″$.

Piecing

Use ¹/₄″ seam allowances. Press seams in the directions indicated by the arrows.

1. Stitch a 17¹/₂″ narrow border strip to each side of the appliquéd center piece. Press toward the narrow borders. Stitch a 19¹/₂″ narrow border strip to the top and bottom of the center. Press toward the narrow borders.

2. Stitch a 19¹/₂″ wide inner-border strip to each side of the quilt top. Press toward the narrow borders. Stitch a 28¹/₂″ wide inner-border strip to the top and bottom of the quilt top. Press toward the narrow borders.

3. Stitch a 28¹/₂″ narrow border strip to each side of the quilt top. Press toward the narrow borders. Stitch a 30¹/₂″ narrow border strip to the top and bottom of the quilt top. Press toward the narrow borders.

4. To make each Shoo-Fly block, stitch 4 white print triangles to 4 blue or red print triangles to form 4 half-square triangle units.

Half-square triangle unit

5. Stitch into rows with 4 white print squares and one blue or red print square. Stitch the rows together. Repeat to make 12 Shoo-Fly blocks.

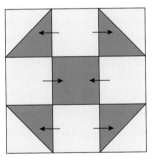

Completed Shoo-Fly block

6. To make the Shoo-Fly border, stitch the Shoo-Fly blocks and the yellow and white check squares together. For the side borders, stitch rows of 2 Shoo-Fly blocks and 3 squares. For the top and bottom borders, stitch rows of 4 Shoo-Fly blocks and 3 squares. Press toward the squares.

7. Stitch the side Shoo-Fly borders to the quilt top. Press toward the narrow borders. Stitch the top and bottom Shoo-Fly borders to the quilt top. Press toward the narrow borders.

8. Stitch a 42¹/₂″ narrow border strip to each side of the quilt top. Press toward the narrow borders. Stitch a 44¹/₂″ narrow border strip to the top and bottom of the quilt top. Press toward the narrow borders.

9. To make the piano key border, stitch the assorted print rectangles together. Stitch 4 rows of 22 rectangles each. Press in one direction.

10. Stitch one row to each side of the quilt top and press toward the narrow borders. Stitch a corner appliquéd piece to each end of the remaining 2 rows. Press away from the corner pieces. Stitch to the top and bottom and press toward the narrow borders.

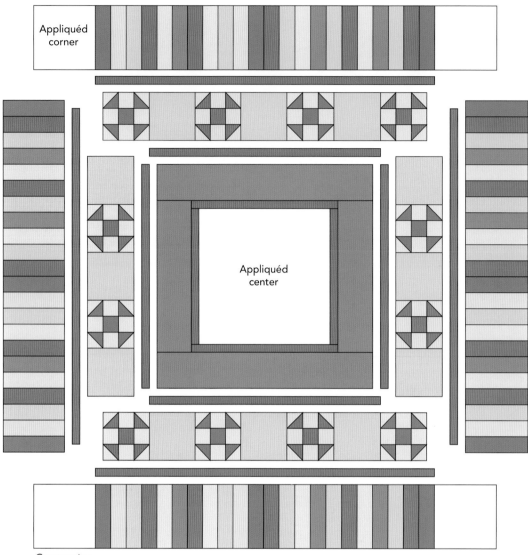

Appliquéd corner

Appliquéd center

Construction

Quilting and Finishing

1. Layer, baste, and quilt your quilt top.

2. Following the instructions on pages 16–17, prepare and stitch 7 strips of binding to the quilt.

Leaf
Cut 6.

Cherry
Cut 11.

Cut 1.

Cut 1.

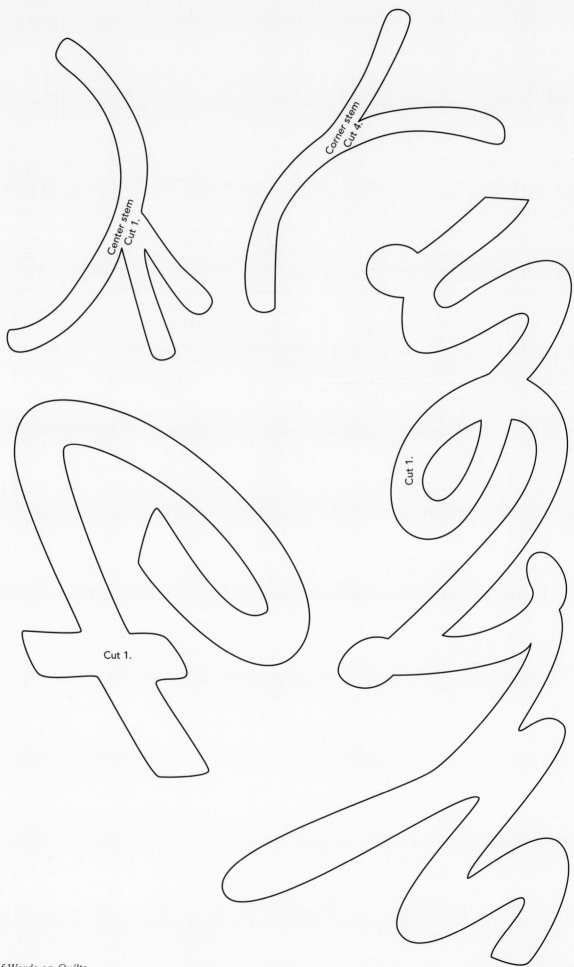

Center stem
Cut 1.

Corner stem
Cut 4.

Cut 1.

Cut 1.

A B C D E
F G H I J K
L M N O P
Q R S T U
V W X Y Z
1 2 3 4 5 6
7 8 9 0

A B C D E F
G H I J K L
M N O P Q
R S T U V
W X Y Z
a b c d e f g h i j
k l m n o p q r s t
u v w x y z 1 2 3
4 5 6 7 8 9 0

A B C D E F G
H I J K L M N
O P Q R S T U
V W X Y Z
a b c d e f g h
i j k l m n o p
q r s t u v w
x y z 1 2 3 4
5 6 7 8 9 0

ABCDEFG
HIJKLMN
OPQRSTU
VWXYZ

abcdefghijkl
mnopqrs
tuvwxyz123
4567890

A B C D E F G
H I J K L M N
O P 2 R S T U
V W X Y 3

a b c d e f g h i j
k l m n o p q r s
t u v w x y z 1 2
3 4 5 6 7 8 9 0

Aa Bb Cc Dd Ee
Ff Gg Hh Ii Jj Kk
Ll Mm Nn Oo Pp
Qq Rr Ss Tt Uu
Vv Ww Xx Yy Zz

1 2 3 4 5 6 7 8 9 0

Sources

The following are some of my favorite sources for fonts.

For computer users:

Broderbund Software
www.broderbund.com
Inexpensive CDs and DVDs containing hundreds of fonts.

Letterhead Fonts
2763 West L Avenue #249
Lancaster, CA 93536
(661) 951-1939
www.letterheadfonts.com
Amazing vintage and retro-style fonts.

Monotype Imaging, Inc.
500 Unicorn Park
Woburn, MA 01801
(800) 424-8973
www.Fonts.com
Enormous selection of fonts in all styles.

P22 Type Foundry
P.O. Box 770
Buffalo, NY 14213
(800) 722-5080
Beautiful fonts that are historically inspired.

Fonts in print:

Dover Publications
31 East 2nd Street
Mineola, NY 11501
www.DoverPublications.com
Dover publishes a large assortment of books of fonts
and some books are available with CDs for use in your
personal computer.

For a list of other fine books from
C&T Publishing, ask for a free catalog:
C&T Publishing, Inc.
P.O. Box 1456
Lafayette, CA 94549
800-284-1114
Email: ctinfo@ctpub.com
Website: www.ctpub.com

For quilting supplies:
Cotton Patch Mail Order
3405 Hall Lane, Dept. CTB
Lafayette, CA 94549
800-835-4418
925-283-7883
Email: quiltusa@yahoo.com
Website: www.quiltusa.com

About the Author

Elizabeth Scott made her first quilt in 1980 and has loved playing with fabric ever since. She also designs patterns under the name *Late Bloomer Quilts* (www.latebloomerquilts.com). Elizabeth lives with her husband, Larry, and three teenage sons Eric, Nick, and Jeff in a very noisy Northern California home.